HOW TO LOOK AFTE

PET CAT

A PRACTICAL GUIDE TO CARING FOR YOUR PET, IN STEP-BY-STEP PHOTOGRAPHS

DAVID ALDERTON

Introduction

Cats, and kittens especially, are cute. However, while they do not need as much care as a dog you must be prepared to spend time every day looking after and playing with a cat. It is also important to take into consideration where you live, before deciding on a cat as a pet. You will need to think about whether it is fair to have a cat if you do not have a garden, particularly if you live next to a busy road. Also remember that cats are long-lived, so you are likely to be choosing a pet who will be with you for perhaps 15 years or more.

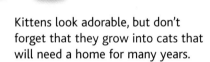

Kittens look adorable, but don't forget that they grow into cats that will need a home for many years.

Getting to know your cat

Your cat will enjoy lots of attention and being played with. As you stroke your cat, you will discover what it likes best. Cats do not like their coat to be stroked from the tail towards the head and many cats do not like having their paws or tummy touched. They do, however, love to have their heads stroked. A kitten will enjoy games, too. Again, you will learn which games it likes the most. Be careful, however, not to overdo it. Always remember that your cat is a living being, and treat it with respect.

What kitten could resist playing with a toy mouse? Don't tease your kitten, though, or it might scratch you.

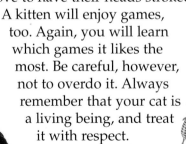

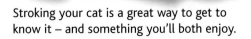

Stroking your cat is a great way to get to know it – and something you'll both enjoy.

Remove your cat from any situation where it might harm other pets.

Family pets

Cats can become friends with dogs, but it helps if they have grown up together, as they are then more likely to get along well. In most homes, it is the cat that is boss. Dogs soon learn to back off if the family cat is hissing and snarling at them. You will need to be very careful if you have other pets, particularly birds or small creatures such as hamsters, because your cat will try to catch and kill them. Never let these animals out of their quarters when your cat is in the same room. If necessary, pick your cat up and remove it from the room first.

Will your pet cat get along with your pet dog? They have a better chance of being friends if they grow up together.

Moggies

The most popular cats as pets are known as moggies or non-pedigrees. They are different from purebred cats, of which there are more than sixty different breeds. Moggies can vary greatly in their appearance, whereas all the cats of a particular breed will look similar to each other. For example, all Siamese cats have both a similar appearance and temperament. Moggies, however, are completely unique.

A moggy may not win the top prizes – but it's bound to win your heart! These cats often have more character and fewer problems than pedigree cats.

What is a cat?

Cats are small furry animals with strong legs, and powerful paws equipped with sharp claws. They are mammals, which are hairy animals with warm blood and babies that drink their mother's milk. The ancestor of today's domestic cats is thought to be the African wild cat that lives in quite dry parts of the world.

Cats are very independent animals but are also devoted to their owners. There are many different breeds, sizes and types to choose from.

A kitten has all the features – including the markings – of the adult cat into which it will grow.

Cat origins

People first began keeping cats in ancient Egypt, over 5,000 years ago. Cats started living in people's homes and for a time were even treated as gods. When they died, people would bury them in large tombs.

Sensing danger

A cat has large ears that are set high on its head, giving it the best chance to pick up sounds. It also has a number of long hairs on its face called whiskers, which allow it to sense if it can squeeze through a gap, such as in a fence, without getting stuck.

Cat's eyes are positioned right at the front of their head so they can see very clearly in front of them, which is very important when they are hunting. As hunters, cats need to be able to see clearly and it helps that they also have good hearing. Cats have sharp teeth so they can hold on to and eat their prey easily.

A cat's important facial features – ears, eyes, teeth and whiskers – are all large.

Ears

Eyes

Teeth

Whiskers

Cat movement

You can tell what kind of mood a cat is in by looking at its tail. When cats are annoyed, they often flick their tails from side to side. They also stretch out their tails behind them when they leap, to help them balance. The hind legs of cats are very strong, which means they can jump very well. If they do start to fall, cats can swivel their bodies round very fast, so they land on their feet, making them less likely to be injured as a result.

A cat is very flexible. It has a bendy skeleton that allows it to stretch up high as well as to curl up into a tight ball.

A cat's tail not only helps it to keep its balance but it also indicates to other cats – and to you – what mood it's in.

This beautiful kitten is a caramel ticked tabby. You can see how its darker markings blend into the paler fur on the rest of its body.

Coat patterning

The pet cats known as tabbies have coat markings called tabby patterning. There are different types: cats that have stripes are known as mackerel tabbies, while others with a large blotch of darker coloration on the sides of their body are called classic tabbies. There are also spotted tabbies, which have spots on their coats, as well as ticked tabbies, where the darker markings merge into the fur. One easy way to recognize all tabbies is by the dark M-shaped pattern in the middle of their forehead. Their tails end in a dark tip, too.

Cat breeds

The first cats kept in Egypt as pets all had short coats. No-one is certain when the first long-haired cats appeared, although it was well over 1,000 years ago. Most of the breeds which come from northern countries have long, thick coats during the winter, to protect them from the cold.

Sphynx

This breed is said to have originated in Central America hundreds of years ago. The Sphynx is furless but its skin is covered with a soft, warm down, which feels like the furred skin of a peach. It is not completely hairless and you may be able to see some hair around the toes, and at the tip of the tail. Sphynx cats are intelligent, very lively and playful.

The Sphynx may be an ideal pet for someone who is usually allergic to cats.

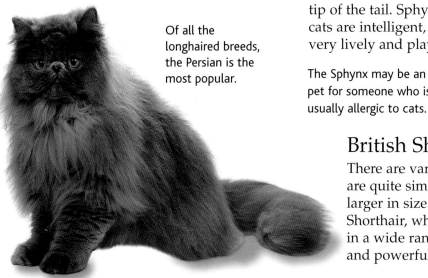

Of all the longhaired breeds, the Persian is the most popular.

British Shorthair

There are various shorthaired breeds that are quite similar to non-pedigrees, but larger in size. They include the British Shorthair, which, like the Persian, is bred in a wide range of hues. They are compact and powerful cats.

Persian Longhair

This is the best-known of all the longhaired breeds. It is bred in many different shades, including pure white. Other pure or "self" colours vary from cream and red to blue, chocolate and black. There are patterned varieties too, including bicolours, which have white areas mixed in their fur. Tortoiseshells, which are often black, red and cream and usually female, are also popular.

British Shorthair cats are admired for their stamina and calm temperament.

Siamese

This is the best-known of the breeds that come from Asia. The Siamese is described as being "pointed", because of the darker fur seen on its points, which are its legs and feet, tail, face and ears. Kittens of the Siamese and similar breeds have pale coats when they are born, and only develop their points as they grow older.

Siamese cats are easily recognized by their piercing blue eyes and their "points".

Ragdoll

While Siamese can be noisy by nature, another "pointed" breed, called the Ragdoll, is considered to be the most gentle of all cats. It relaxes in your arms, and goes limp like a toy ragdoll when picked up.

The Ragdoll is a large, heavy cat with medium-length fur and blue eyes.

Devon Rex

There are a number of breeds of cat that have thin, curly coats. These are known as rexed cats. The Devon Rex, which has a pixie-like look, is one of the most popular.

The Devon Rex has a distinctive head shape with huge ears.

The Maine Coon's luxurious fur needs daily grooming.

Maine Coon

The oldest breed from North America, the Maine coon was bred from cats brought from Europe by settlers over 300 years ago. It is one of the world's largest breeds, being bigger than some small dogs.

Choosing your cat

If you are seeking a kitten of a particular breed, you may not be able to obtain your new pet until it is at least 12 weeks old. These kittens develop more slowly than ordinary moggies, which are usually old enough to go to a new home from eight weeks of age onwards. It will not matter too much whether the kitten you have chosen is a male, called a tom, or a female, which is described as a queen. If cats are neutered there is little difference in behaviour between a male and a female cat.

Choose a kitten that is bright and lively. Make sure their eyes are clear, there is no staining under the tail and that they can move around freely.

Where to go

If you are looking for a particular breed, then you will need to track down a breeder. This can usually be done through advertisements in cat magazines or at a cat show, or through the Internet if you cannot visit a show. If you are searching for a moggie, however, it should be much easier and cheaper to acquire a kitten, perhaps from a friend or through an animal rescue organization.

Animal rescue organizations tend to have more adult cats to find homes for than cute, cuddly kittens. However, you may strike lucky!

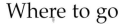

An older cat

Most people want to start off with a kitten, but you may want to think about giving a home to an older cat. These are sometimes handed in to rescue centres because their owners are moving and cannot take their pets with them. Older cats, which are used to people, can settle well in new homes, and become just as friendly as kittens.

An older cat will probably feel just as relaxed and comfortable in its new home as a kitten will.

One or two cats?

A cat can live very happily on its own. Cats are not especially friendly towards each other, unless they have grown up together. If you want to have two, therefore, it is a good idea to obtain them at the same time, when they are both kittens.

Cats that have grown up in a household together usually get on well.

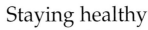

You'll need a carrying basket to take your cat to the vet.

Staying healthy

Always ask the person from whom you obtain your cat if it has already had its vaccinations, as these are very important to protect your pet from illnesses that can otherwise kill it. If your new pet has been vaccinated already, be sure to ask for the vaccination certificate. Deworming is also very important. This is something you will need to speak to your vet about, when you take your pet for its first check-up.

Your cat's home

It is a good idea to prepare everything – such as bedding, a litter box, food bowls and toys – before you go to collect your new pet. You will need to plan where in the home you are going to keep your kitten, as it will not be safe to let your new pet out straight away. Kittens must be kept indoors until after they have completed their course of vaccinations, because otherwise they could catch a serious illness. If you have chosen an older cat, you must keep it indoors for at least two weeks – if you let it out it is likely to wander off in search of its old home.

This bed is the height of cat luxury – but an old cardboard box will do just as well.

Whatever the age of the cat you choose, it will need to be kept indoors at first for at least two weeks, until there is no danger that it will try to find its way back to its old home.

Your cat's bed

Make sure your cat has its own bed placed in a quiet, warm corner of your home. Just a simple cardboard box lined with a blanket will do, or you can buy a special cat bed from a pet store, but most cats will sleep just about anywhere. If you acquire a kitten, make sure that the bed you provide will be large enough when your cat is fully grown. Don't let your cat into your bedroom as it may go to the toilet there or fall asleep on the bed. If your cat is carrying any fleas these may be left on your bed.

Danger!

There are a number of possible dangers that could injure your pet. Cats will often jump up on to work surfaces, and can burn themselves badly if they accidentally walk across the hot rings of a cooker. Especially in the summer, be sure that the doors to any upstairs rooms are closed when your cat or kitten is roaming around the home. Otherwise, your pet may sneak out through an open window or on to a balcony. Young cats, especially, can fall and injure themselves seriously, as their sense of balance is not as good as an adult cat's.

Although the back of the cooker seems like a nice, warm place for a cat to sit, it is highly dangerous and should be discouraged.

When you bring your cat home, try to bring a toy from its former home if you can, to make your pet feel more secure.

Play time

Set aside time every day to play with your pet. There are many different types of toy that you can buy in pet stores for cats of all ages. You will soon discover which your pet likes best. Never tease your cat when playing, because this may end up with you being scratched or bitten as a result. If your cat lives only indoors, a play area that includes a climbing frame and a scratching post is a very good idea.

Be gentle when playing with a kitten and you will find that you have made a friend for the rest of its life.

Feeding and training

All cats are carnivores, which means they eat meat and fish, and cannot be fed on vegetarian food. There are plenty of special foods for cats that are available from supermarkets and pet stores. These foods come in different forms. Canned food, which looks most like meat, is often a cat's preference, but they will eat semi-moist and dry foods too. It helps to give a range of these foods to a young cat, so that it will not be fussy about its food later in life.

You may find that dried food is often a more convenient way to feed your pet than with canned food.

Kittens should be fed special kitten food. You can get this from a supermarket or a pet store.

How much food?

If you are giving packet food, all you need to do is to pour the correct amount into your pet's bowl. There are special foods of this type for kittens, as well as for older cats. You will soon know how much your cat will eat on a regular basis, but you can also work this out from the information on the packaging. It is better just to give your pet the amount that it will eat within a few minutes, rather than tipping a larger amount into its food bowl, as this can encourage a cat to eat too much. This in turn means that your cat is likely to become overweight before long. If you are feeding an adult cat canned food, you will find that it will probably eat about one large can per day, in two meals.

Milk or water?

All cats need to have a clean bowl of drinking water available at all times, but it is not necessary to give your pet milk. Some cats, especially Siamese, cannot digest cow's milk, which causes them to have diarrhoea. Specially-made milk for cats that will not have this effect can be purchased at pet stores.

Your cat does not need milk – but it does need a bowl of fresh water available at all times.

The litter box

You will need a litter box where your cat can go to the toilet. Line the litter box with newspaper and pour cat litter on top. If you place your kitten here when it is most likely to want to use the box, usually after a meal, you should not have any accidents around the home. (However, your kitten may mistake dry food for litter.) Wear plastic gloves when you change the soiled litter and tip it into a plastic bag. Wash your hands afterwards.

1 Line your cat's litter box with newspaper and pour cat litter on top.

2 Carefully lift up your kitten and put it in the litter box after it has eaten a meal.

3 Stop your kitten from climbing out, to try and encourage it to use the box for going to the toilet.

Grooming and handling

Cats often enjoy being groomed, especially once they become used to having their coat combed and brushed. Long-haired cats can be more difficult to groom than short-hairs, however, so it is important to start this process while your cat is still young. At this age, their coats are still quite short and are less likely to become matted. If they do become knotted, then just as with your own hair, grooming can become extremely painful. Your cat may try to scratch you and run away as a result.

An adult long-haired cat will need to be groomed every day to avoid its coat becoming matted.

Picking up your cat

Cats are not difficult to pick up, especially when they are young. Place one hand around its tummy and then lift up its hind quarters. Always support the underside of your cat's body, because if the cat feels that it might fall, then it is likely to scratch you. It is a good idea to ask an adult to show you how to lift up a cat safely, so you know what to do. Remember that some adult cats are quite heavy, which can make them difficult to handle.

Stroking your cat regularly helps to remove loose hairs and keeps your cat's coat shiny.

Pick your cat up regularly so that it gets used to being handled in this way.

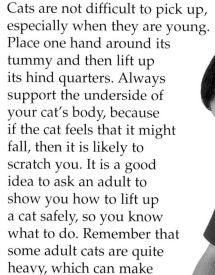

Grooming tools

You will need a brush and comb for your cat. It helps if you buy a comb with revolving teeth, so that if any mats do form in the coat, this will help to tease them apart, rather than pulling them, which will be painful for the cat. Rexes do not require much grooming. Owners often need only stroke their cats' fur with a piece of silk, to keep it looking glossy.

Looking for problems

If you look carefully at the coat of your cat when stroking it, you may see the short down hair, which acts like a vest to keep the cat warm, and the longer outer hairs. Watch for dark specks, which may be flea droppings, or even fleas running through the fur. If your cat has fleas, you should use a special fine-toothed comb, and a flea collar or powder – ask an adult to help with this – or take it to the vet.

Loose hair

It is really important to remove the loose hair because otherwise your cat may swallow these hairs when it licks its coat. Hairs stick to the cat's tongue, and then are swallowed, causing a blockage in the stomach known as a fur ball. A cat will stop eating as much as usual and may look run down if it is suffering from a furball. Cats bring up fur balls unless they become stuck – if this happens take your cat to the vet.

Brushing and combing your cat

Short-haired cats will need to be combed and brushed in the direction of their fur, but in the case of long-haireds, brush backwards first, lifting the coat up, before combing it down again. In the spring, cats shed more of their coat, a process called moulting. Some long-haireds will then resemble short-haireds through the summer months, although the fur on their tails always remains longer.

A comb with revolving teeth is much less painful for your cat when you tease out any knotted fur.

Always brush a short-haired cat in the direction of its fur.

Cats out of doors

Most cats like to wander outdoors, but there is a risk that they could be run over by traffic. Since accidents of this type often happen at night, you should always encourage your cat to come indoors at this time. During the day when you are not there, you can allow your cat to wander in and out through its own special door, known as a cat flap. You can fit your cat with a magnet on an elasticated collar, which acts rather like a key. This means that only your cat can enter your home, rather than other cats in the area, who might steal your pet's food or mess up your home.

A cat flap lets your pet come in and out of the house as it pleases.

Neutering your cat

Tom cats that are not neutered are likely to stray and become involved in fights, while unneutered female cats will soon become pregnant with unwanted kittens. These problems can be prevented if your pet is neutered by your vet when it is between four and six months of age.

Nature's hunters

It is upsetting when a cat catches a bird or a butterfly, but your pet is a hunter by nature, and scolding is unlikely to have any effect. Instead, try fitting a bell on an elasticated collar, which will warn birds of your pet's presence nearby, allowing them to fly away to safety.

A simple way to stop your cat bringing home dead birds and mice is to fit its collar with a bell.

To prevent your female cat from becoming pregnant you should have it neutered when it is still young.

Avoiding conflict

Cats living in towns live much closer together than their wild ancestors. If you watch other cats in the local area, as well as your own, you will see how they follow particular paths to avoid coming into conflict with each other.

Cats are very attracted to catnip, after sniffing it some cats will roll around in happiness.

Many cats cannot resist a toy that has been scented with catnip.

A cat's best-loved herb

Catnip causes a strong reaction in many cats. After sniffing catnip, many cats will roll around on the ground, appearing very happy. Not all of them respond in this way, however, nor do young kittens. Some toys are scented with catnip, to make them more attractive to cats.

Hot weather

Try not to allow your cat to stay outside when the sun is very hot, because your pet can become sunburned. Cats with white fur, especially on their ears, are very vulnerable and may even develop skin cancer from being repeatedly burned on this part of their body.

Your cat will almost certainly enjoy sunbathing, but beware of very hot weather, when cats, especially those with white fur, can get sunburned.

Going on holiday

It is not a good idea to take your cat on holiday with you, even if you are just going a short distance by car, as cats do not like to travel. You could ask a friend to visit while you are away, to give your cat fresh food and water, but there is always a risk that your cat might wander off and disappear.

If you leave your cat in a cattery, remember to provide any special foods that your cat needs.

Make sure you leave plenty of time to catch your cat before setting off for the cattery!

Cat to the cattery

The best way to make sure your cat is safe while you're on holiday is to book it into a cattery. You will need to make arrangements for your cat well in advance, as soon as you know when you will be away. Otherwise, you may find that there are no vacancies, especially during busy holiday periods. Arrange to take your cat to the cattery the day before you leave. Otherwise, if you cannot find your pet on the day you are due to go, you may unfortunately be delayed in leaving.

Fit and healthy

Most cats rarely fall ill, but you must keep their vaccinations up to date. Once the initial course of injections has been completed, around 12 weeks of age, your cat is then likely to need annual booster jabs. These protect your pet against serious illnesses such as cat flu.

Worming tablets

Cats can suffer from various worms in their digestive system, which they pick up when hunting or even from fleas. These need to be treated regularly using special tablets which have to be dropped directly into your cat's mouth. It is best to ask your vet or an adult to do this for you as it may not be as easy as it sounds. Tilt the cat's head well back, before carefully opening its mouth so it will swallow the tablet properly.

1 Hold the cat steady and tilt the cat's head well back. Then carefully open its mouth and pop the tablet in.

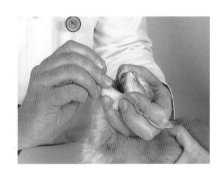

2 Hold the cat's mouth closed. Then stroke its throat to make sure that it swallows the tablet. When the cat licks its lips it has swallowed the pill.

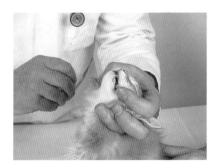

Signs of illness

Cats sometimes fight and may develop a swelling known as an abscess after being bitten. This is likely to need veterinary attention. Also, contact your vet if your cat loses its appetite or appears to have difficulty in walking, or if its third eyelid appears across the corner of the eye, which is a sign that your cat is poorly.

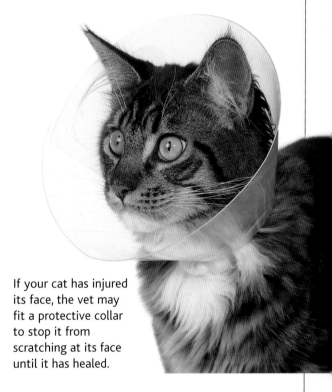

If your cat has injured its face, the vet may fit a protective collar to stop it from scratching at its face until it has healed.

Old age

As cats get older, their breath often smells unpleasant. This can be because their teeth need cleaning, or because their kidneys are not working as well as when they were younger. Old cats should be taken for a check-up at the vet's every six months or so as a precaution.

This edition is published by Armadillo, an imprint of Anness Publishing Ltd, Blaby Road, Wigston, Leicestershire LE18 4SE; info@anness.com

www.annesspublishing.com

If you like the images in this book and would like to investigate using them for publishing, promotions or advertising, please visit our website www.practicalpictures.com for more information.

Publisher: Joanna Lorenz
Editor: Sarah Uttridge
Designer: Linda Penny
Photographer: Paul Bricknell
Production Controller: Pirong Wang

The publishers would also like to thank Grace Crissell, Olivia Martin-Simons and Sam Martin-Simons for appearing in this book.

A CIP catalogue record for this book is available from the British Library.

PUBLISHER'S NOTE
Although the advice and information in this book are believed to be accurate and true at the time of going to press, neither the authors nor the publisher can accept any legal responsibility or liability for any errors or omissions that may have been made nor for any inaccuracies nor for any loss, harm or injury that comes about from following instructions or advice in this book.

Manufacturer: Anness Publishing Ltd, Blaby Road, Wigston, Leicestershire LE18 4SE, England
For Product Tracking go to: www.annesspublishing.com/tracking
Batch: 2914-22317-1127